Awful, Disgusting Parasites

ROUND WORMS

BARBARA CILETTI

BLACK
RABBIT
BOOKS

Bolt is published by Black Rabbit Books
P.O. Box 3263, Mankato, Minnesota, 56002.
www.blackrabbitbooks.com
Copyright © 2017 Black Rabbit Books

Design and Production by Michael Sellner
Photo Research by Rhonda Milbrett

Library of Congress Control Number: 2015954682

HC ISBN: 978-1-68072-009-9   PB ISBN: 978-1-68072-273-4

Printed in the United States at CG Book Printers,
North Mankato, Minnesota, 56003. PO #1792 4/16

Web addresses included in this book were working and appropriate
at the time of publication. The publisher is not responsible for broken
or changed links.

Image Credits

Corbis: David Scharf/Corbis,
Cover; David Mccarthy/Science Photo
Library, 3, 12; Dr. Richard Kessel & Dr. Gene
Shih/Visuals Unlimited, Back Cover, 1, 16–17
(background); Dreamstime: Science Pics, 25 (mid-
dle); istock: BeholdingEye, 17 (top), 24; medicalook.
com: 6–7; Science Source, Claude Nuridsany & Marie
Perennou, 4–5; SciePro, 6, 15, 25 (top), 29, 31; Shutter-
stock: alexnika, 23; Andrey_Kuzmin, 25 (bottom); Desig-
nua, 9; Jiri Hera, 27 (bottom); Marcel Jancovic, 10–11;
Margoe Edwards, 27 (top); Morphart Creation, 20–21
(background); rangizzz, 17 (bottom); showcake, 16; The
Len, 11; Yavuz Sariyildiz, 19; Superstock: NHPA/Photo-
shot/Photoshot, 14; Wikimedia: Allen Jefthas, 22, 32
Every effort has been made to contact copyright
holders for material reproduced in this book.
Any omissions will be rectified in subse-
quent printings if notice is given to
the publisher.

Contents

CHAPTER 1

Unexpected

Lunch Date

A woman took a bite of her lunch. She didn't wash her hands first. She thought her hands were clean. But hiding on her hands were tiny eggs. She didn't know it, but she ate those eggs with her lunch.

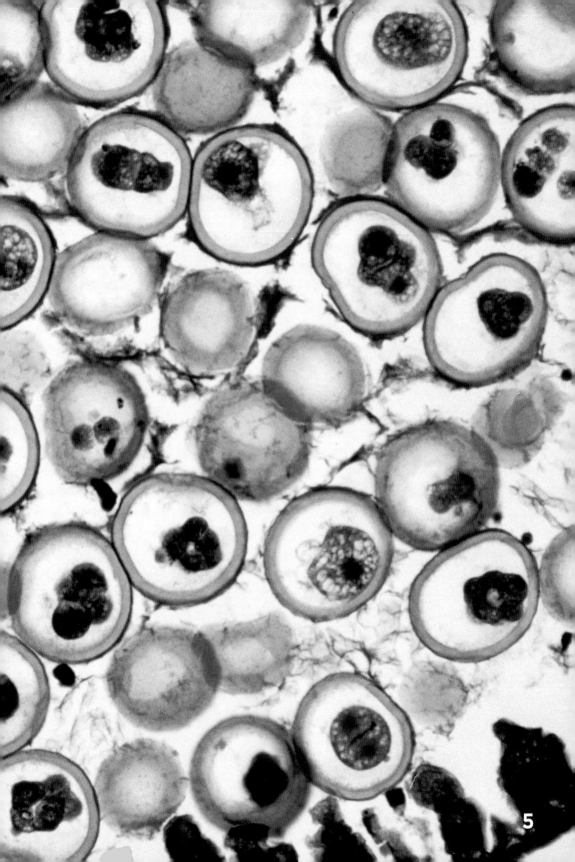

5

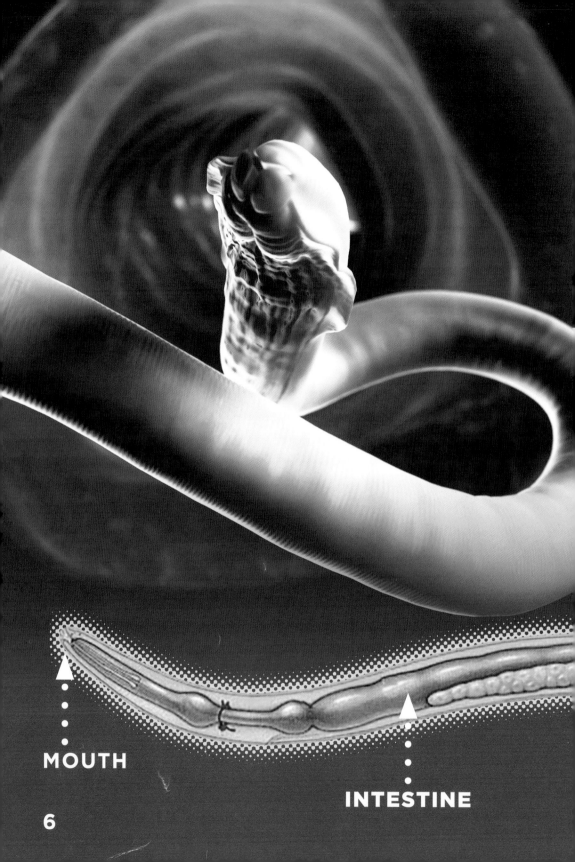

MOUTH

INTESTINE

6

Worms in the Body

Inside the woman's body, the eggs grew into roundworms. Roundworms are **parasites** that live and feed on people and other animals. These worms are gross. And they can make people very sick.

Roundworm Parts

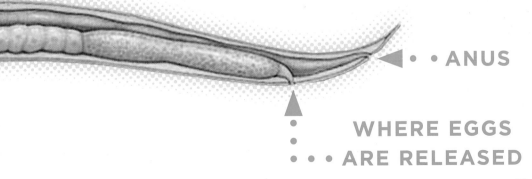

◄ • • ANUS

WHERE EGGS
ARE RELEASED

Roundworm Symptoms

People with roundworms might have some **symptoms**. Other people won't feel any different.

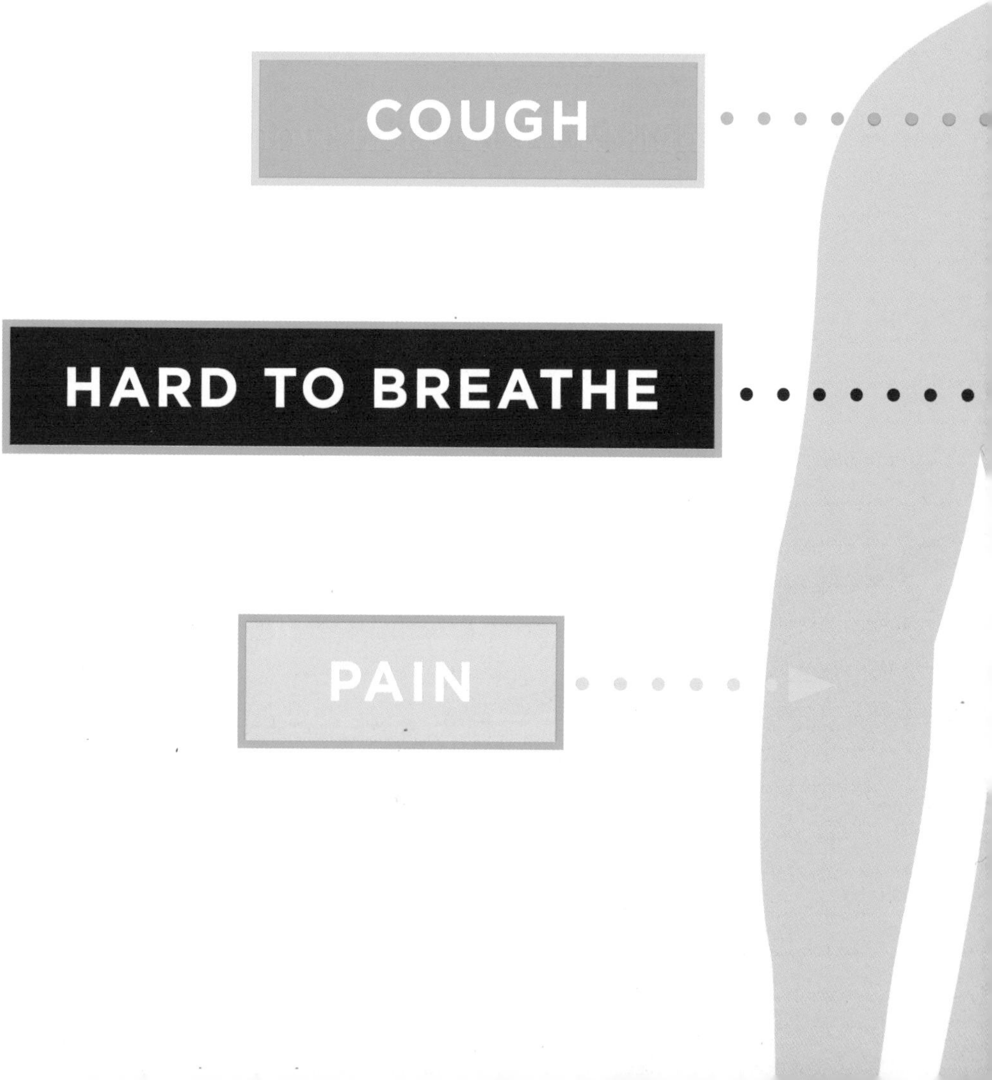

COUGH

HARD TO BREATHE

PAIN

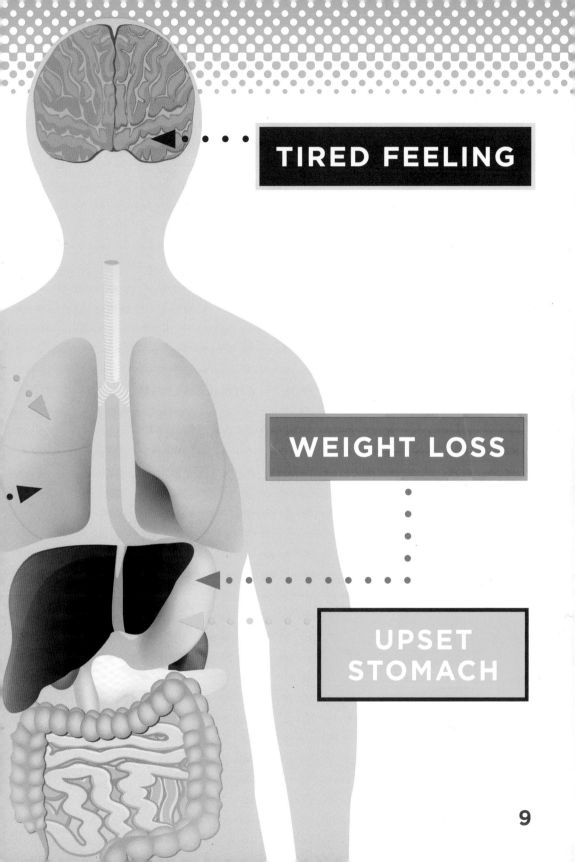

TIRED FEELING

WEIGHT LOSS

UPSET STOMACH

9

CHAPTER 2

Tricky Travelers

Roundworm eggs live in dirt. The eggs are so small, they are nearly invisible. When people work in the dirt, they can't see the eggs. If they touch their dirty hands to their mouths, they could swallow the eggs.

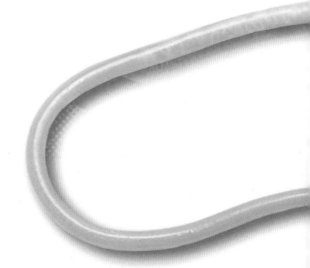

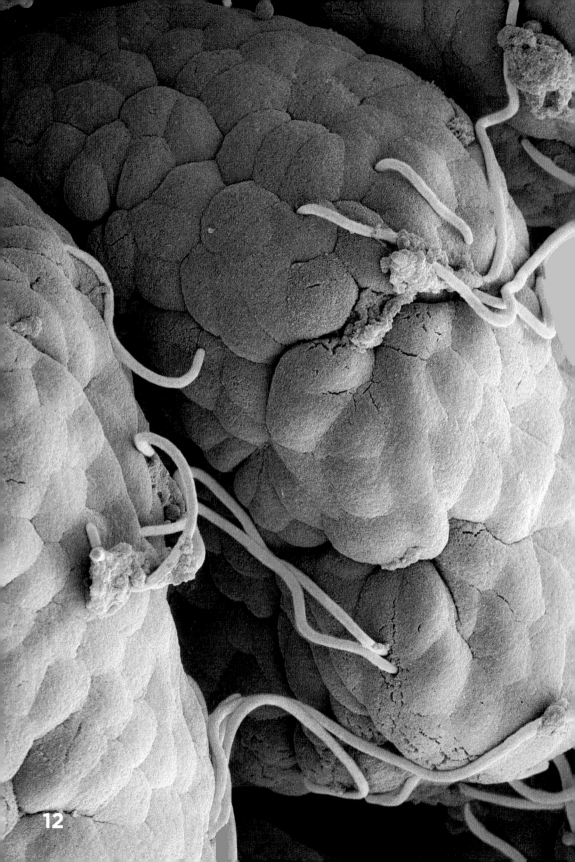

Coughed Up

Inside a body, the eggs travel to the intestines. There, the eggs hatch. The roundworms then dig themselves out of the intestines. They travel to the **lungs**.

In the lungs, the roundworms cause the person to cough. Coughing pushes the worms into the throat. When the person swallows, the worms go to the intestines again.

Growing

Inside a person, roundworms eat and grow. They eat partly **digested** food.

Once they're grown, adult roundworms lay eggs. The eggs leave a person's body with his or her poop.

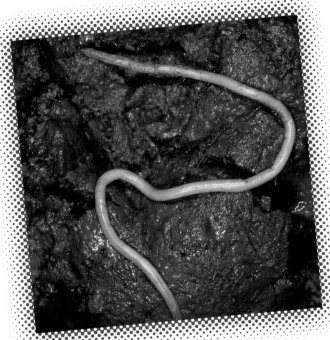

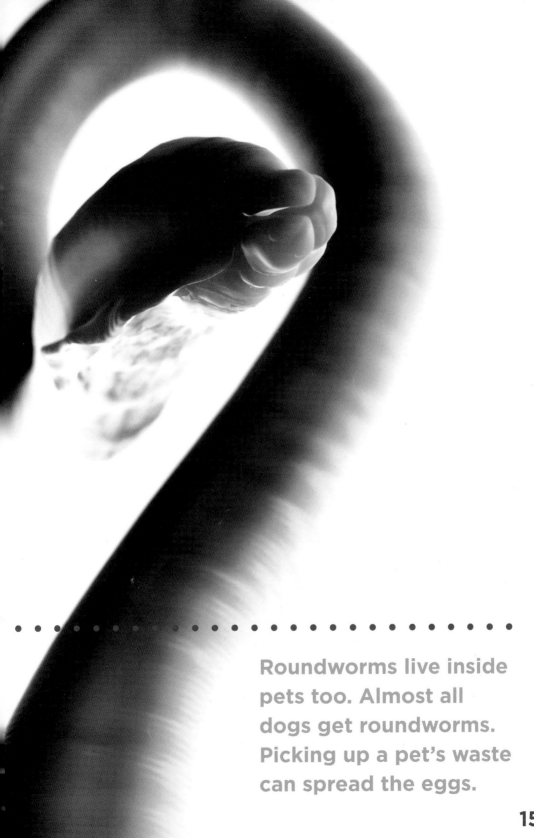

Roundworms live inside pets too. Almost all dogs get roundworms. Picking up a pet's waste can spread the eggs.

PEOPLE AND ANIMALS

People or animals pick up the eggs by touching the dirt.

EGGS

Eggs grow inside
a body. Adult roundworms
then make new eggs.

DIRT

The eggs leave the body through
poop. The eggs live in the dirt.

CHAPTER 3

Home Sweet Home

Roundworms live all around the world. They are most often found in places with warm weather.

These parasites spread quickly in areas without good bathrooms. In some poor areas, people poop and pee on the ground. In these places, it's easy to pick up roundworm eggs.

Treating Roundworms

Roundworms make millions of people sick every year. Doctors have medications that help. These medications kill the parasites. In some cases, people might need **surgery** to remove the worms.

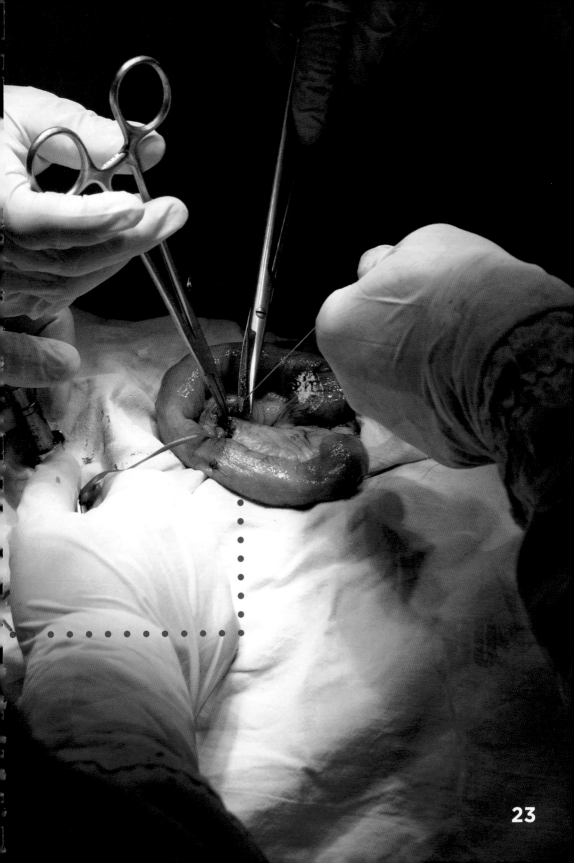

By the Numbers

200,000
number of eggs laid by a female every day

20,000
number of people who die from roundworms each year

2
years a roundworm can live in a person

up to
1 BILLION
number of people who get worms every year

3 FEET
(1 M)

length of one kind of roundworm

most roundworms grow up to **20** inches (51 cm) long

CHAPTER 4

Prevention

Avoiding roundworms is the best way to stop them. People should clean their hands before eating. And always wash up after using the bathroom.

Roundworm parasites are troublemakers. But don't fear. With clean hands and clean food, people can be worm free!

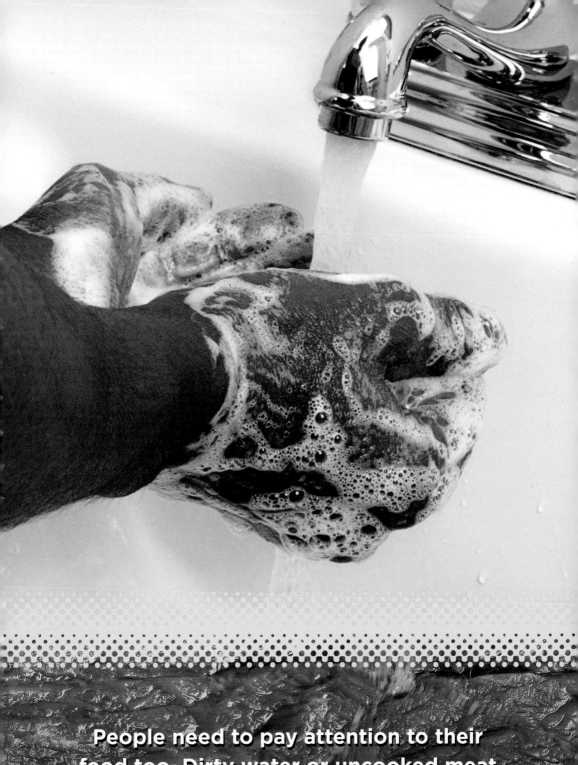

People need to pay attention to their food too. Dirty water or uncooked meat can carry roundworm eggs.

Crazy Roundworms

More than 15,000 types of roundworms live in the world. But they are all amazing. Did you know:

- roundworms have no backbones?
- these parasites can live in freshwater and salt water?
- they have teeth to bite food?

avoid (uh-VOYD)—to keep away from

digest (dy-JEST)—to change the food eaten into a form that can be used by the body

intestine (en-TE-sten)—the part of the digestive system where most food is digested; in humans, it is a long tube made up of the small intestine and the large intestine.

lung (LUNG)—an organ in the body used for breathing; most people have two lungs.

parasite (PAR-uh-syt)—a plant or animal that lives in or on another plant or animal and gets its food or protection from it

surgery (SURJ-ree)—a medical treatment where a doctor cuts into someone's body to fix something

symptom (SYMP-tuhm)—a change in the mind or body that means a disease is present

BOOKS

Albee, Sarah. *Bugged: How Insects Changed History.* New York: Bloomsbury/Walker, 2014.

Gomdori co. *Survive! Inside the Human Body. Vol. 1: The Digestive System.* San Francisco: No Starch Press, 2013.

Murawski, Darlyne, and Nancy Honovich. *Ultimate Bug-Opedia: The Most Complete Bug Reference Ever.* Washington, D.C.: National Geographic, 2013.

WEBSITES

Ascariasis
kidshealth.org/parent/infections/stomach/ascariasis.html

Roundworm
encyclopedia.kids.net.au/page/ro/Roundworm

Roundworms Have the Right Stuff
science.nasa.gov/science-news/science-at-nasa/2015/23may_roundworms/

INDEX